Praise for Richard Jackson's Previous Books

I think he is either the god Hermes or a sparrow. He is certainly a messenger. And what he says is contained in a single word, although it comes out as amazement, anger, joy, sadness, in an astounding cascade of images, and a variety of tongues. He is a poet of great sweep and vision. He is deeply tender. He is a master of music, one of our finest poets.
—Gerald Stern

Richard Jackson has become one of our most important poets. His subjects are those for which poetry originally came into being. The essentials are his songs, his precepts, his adoration. It isn't simply solace he offers, but it's solace nevertheless that he lends us.
—James Tate

His lines are clouds of love, piercing the sky with enormous empathy, rolling in the azure, torrents of passion, and are arrows at the same time, reaching a peak where they break, crying, cleansing the air, becoming ether. It is impossible to describe this in discursive language. With a melody that is unmistakably his own...he is a kind of Scorsese in poetry, but where Scorsese almost succeeds in his films, then stops, seals and terrifies us, Jackson adds a tender, vulnerable voice that blossoms and transforms us and that is so unique and great, great in its truest sense in Richard Jackson's poetry.
—Tomaž Šalamur

D1253239

What you find in Richard Jackson's great heart and spirit is poetry of generosity and fearless attention you won't find anywhere else.
—Dara Wier

The wonderful amplitude of the poems, their teeming grace, testifies that we can live with such chaos and not lie about it or ignore it; indeed the poems are a demonstration of how we might do such a thing.
—William Matthews

In its range of emotions, its rich ruminating prosody, in its capacity to contain all that it imagines, and especially in its power to place the corruptions of the world against those of the heart, it represents a poetry of scale, in fine yet compelling excess, informed—indeed exalted, by intelligence, irony and vision.
—Stanley Plumly

Dispatches

Richard Jackson

Wet Cement Press
Berkeley, California

ISBN: 979-8-9856206-3-4

Cover image: "I've seen a dying star" from Metka Krašovec's Emily Dickinson series of drawings; 18x15 mm.

Thanks to the following publications where some of these poems first appeared: Ljubljana Diary and Ljubliana Fifties first appeared in *Strays* (Foundlings Press limited edition chapbook). How to Live, What to Do, Suburban Morning, Elementary Cosmology, Belief, Two Galaxies, The Perseids, Complimentarity, Another Farewell to Truth, Syrian Elegy, Nightly News and The Keys appeared in *Take Five* (Finishing Line Press). The Map of Grief appeared in *Miramar Magazine*

Wet Cement Press
1908 Yolo Ave
Berkeley, California 94707

www.wetementpress.com

Dispatches

Watching the first sunlight
touch the tops of the palms
what could I ask
—*WS Merwin*

Now we are all sitting here strangely
On top of the sunlight.
—*James Wright*

MEDITATIONS IN TROUBLED TIMES

ANOTHER FAREWELL TO TRUTH

Politics can no longer be thought of in terms of truth.
—Gianni Vattimo

The late sun bleeds its own light across the surface of the water. A yellow butterfly sips a little life from the edge. Someone has left an out of date history book on the bank. Beyond these hills the winds are trying to decide who controls the dust they kick up out of the ruins they have made. The tiny lizard with its tail chewed off has a question we'll never hear. A cloud of gnats keeps shifting direction over the surface. Each evening I understand less of why we are here. It is as if our shadows slipped downstream without us.

Crossville Scene

Where is it one first heard of the truth? The the.
      —Wallace Stevens, "The Man on the Dump"

A wet leaf struggles across the pavement as if it were a mouse or a mole guided by a wind made visible by the mist. It passes a man having lunch from a dumpster behind the supermarket. The skeletal trees seem to frown on this wind that tugs at the man's coat. There's something it is trying to tell him. He stuffs a wrapper in his pocket for later. If he had words for it, he would answer the wind. The day already feels used. The rain keeps prodding whatever it will. Is there anything more? Did you think there was a moral here, or that the wind would have something to say to us?

Crossville TN

NOTHING AT ALL

It is therefore senseless to think of complaining since nothing foreign has decided what we feel, what we live, or what we are.

—Jean-Paul Sartre, *Being and Nothingness*

You think you have been here before, and time starts to wobble on its axis. The path you are on is not the path you are on. The robin can't find its nest. There are sounds with no source, roots that lose their way and break the surface. There, in the middle of the woods, is a stone wall that stretches fifty feet but marks nothing, belongs to nothing, stands for nothing. In the distance a shaft of light falls on nothing in particular. There is nothing to say, nothing to do, nowhere to go. Your own watch stutters its alarm.

COMPLIMENTARITY

*How, in physics, two opposite things can be true
at once.*

Thinking he is alone in the park he thinks of
the mind as a seesaw where the two children
rock back and forth. On the one side he is
still alone in the park, on the other side he
rises above even himself. In that version he sits
alone with the buzzard in a dying maple. This
is not the world he wanted to escape into. The
day wears itself out like a used toy. The wind
twists through the trees. One thought follows
another with relentless regularity. He wants to
erase himself into another future. This is when
he calls upon us, because it is we who have been
thinking this. The mind is a clone of itself.

Fog Rises from the Leaves

Like a blossom, like an empty mouth / I go.
—Tomaž Šalamun

Through the barren tree limbs and the fog that
lingers like a half remembered thought, the
moon is a bright smudge that hides whatever
stars were around it. But nothing is ever where
or when we see it. I remember the flashlights
fingering their way through ground fog as we
searched for Ludwig. Lipica. When was that?
Leaves are scattered on the ground like unused
words. Gravitational waves bend the light, and
time. Maybe that is why the child asked today,
when we lose time can we find it later? Tonight
it is almost two years. Galaxies continue to
flow in currents and swirl in eddies like pools
of water the child was playing in. There's a face
in every word we remember. That's why your
own words echo here tonight. *Megla se dviga
iz listja. Fog rises from the leaves. Utrujen sem
biti sam. I am tired of being alone.* Every word
has a future tense the way Zechariah's horses
and trees stood for future worlds he couldn't
see. Today we are still trying to map the cosmos
though its pages are smeared with theories.
And who are we but metaphors for what we
want to be?

Nightly News

Your burn in one place, then you burn in another.
— Gerald Stern, "The World We Should Have
Stayed In"

Twilight spies on us from the tops of the pines.
A few unidentified sounds break in from the
growing darkness. Someone says we are not safe
here. Someone says the moment has already
been stolen. Vapor trails crisscross like broken
branches. They have nothing to do with the
news of the huge tube-shaped asteroid heading
our way. Our own wishes limp for cover. On
their way to us the stories die as they always
do here. In a little while the yellow crime scene
tape will wrap their words as evidence for what
they did not say in time.

THE MAP OF GRIEF

Man, when he does not grieve, hardly exists.
                —Antonio Porchia, *Voces*, 1943

There's a looming quiet as even the insects pause while we pass. Clouds try to reinvent themselves but remain as clouds. The space around us opens like a flower until we seem to walk in a world beyond this one. In everything seen there is something unseen. The dried mud patches written over by horses form little dunes. Around us the treefall has left the air splintered. You can almost smell time in the dirt. It has been over a year now. Then suddenly a white moth crosses the patch, shattering the silence, waving its message like a signal flag in a language only the dead can read. Such is the relief map of grief.

THE KEYS

I want to possess the atoms of time.
> —Clarice Lispector, *Agua Viva*

As the earth turns away from the sun, a few cumulous clouds glow gold at the edges promising what they can't deliver. Another darkness sifts down upon us. The last chimney swifts take their secrets back to their own darkness. There are still a few signs to decipher. The crickets adjust our watches by the weather. The spider maps our universe further than we can see. The moth at the lamp reads our future in the directions the flame jabs. On the new mown field two rabbits face off, then jump over each in some coded way until they scamper into the underbrush. Do you think I meant these as metaphors for what we don't know? No, I am sitting here with grief, with this set of keys left by a dead man that were never intended to open any doors.

DISPATCHES

SHADOWS

It is true, that star you see is really a galaxy, and its beam of light shadows a million stories. And it is true that the reflections now buried in the lake are the shadowy stories of history that no one wants to hear. Those flowers that never had a chance to bud have no words to say what they meant. Everything, every word, harbors a history it later denies. *Our Culture*, for instance, means what hovered over those it enslaved or oppressed. Sometimes even our brightest hopes appear like negatives on a film. The couple we watched from afar walking towards the woods this evening with their heavy knapsacks were not hikers at all but carried their whole lives towards a shelter hidden in the shadows of trees. Our words for this shimmer like the sun's corona blotted out by a full eclipse. For the men living in the boarded-up house who have turned into their own shadows, for the child we read about shot by a stray shadow where she slept, for the shadows on the lungs of politicians that spread like oil spills across the bay, our own silences spill over like black lava fields. And so it is we sit apart with our own misshapen shadows that no longer resemble us.

Unsayable

You try to find a word, a metaphor for it—
the rust destroying the rose bush, the odor of
decay in the compost, the grotesque masks
we put on our histories, the church graveyard
with its unanswered questions, the cauldron
of terror each shimmering star hides, but
nothing compares to the feeling you get for the
room where the Yemeni child dying for lack
of medicine, amuses herself by playing feeble
shadow puppets against the molding hospital
wall.

READING PLATO AT A CABIN IN CROSSVILLE

...and all our thoughts are a dream.
                    —Plato

Some dreams dream on without us and we hear
them like the background phone ringing from
the TV, the trucks' gear shifts from the distant
highway, the saxophone's last note barely
hanging on, or, beyond this window, the prayer
that seems to hover over the deer as they step
deeper towards the woods grazing on darkness,
or the silence that is the thistle light of their
eyes staring back, for whatever we dream means
something more, an idea so beautiful the deer
abandon whatever words I have invented for
them and turn to graze for herbs, salt grass,
greenwood, sometimes springing suddenly,
whistling, as they will, in a language of fear or
surprise.

How to Live, What to Do

There was the man playing his invisible violin on the street corner this morning, the roofers racing against the coming storm, the geese concerned with the right formation, the boy sling-shotting pigeons in the park, the man tasting his vintage cabernet, all in the midst of dreams that float like feathers from a bird the cats have caught, sayings that leak meanings they never intended, numbers too large to reveal what they hide like the Syrian homeless hiding beneath the shattered shells of their homes, and there is this box turtle eating the grapes I've left for him, circling the house like a planet or moon, though every moment contains all time for him as he follows star maps he's traced on the inside of his shell, whole constellations that lead him from one story to another, stories that say, yes, you can notice also this, the way the grass rises again after your step, how the rose petal leaves its sheen between your fingers, how the wind brings tickets for journeys hidden in words you have not yet discovered, stories that teach you it is all right to love the world again.

ELEMENTARY COSMOLOGY

All of this happened when I knocked down the abandoned paper wasp nest, amazed at all the tunnels once crowded with workers heading towards a single center, a kind of geometry I once read for parallel worlds like the Koch Snowflake made by adding triangles at different angles so the center holds constant while the circumference, in infinite divisions, moves forever towards eternity, something our words try hopelessly to cast a net over, the mystery of this, the love of it, geese in formation, mustangs moving in a single wave, chimney swifts like a single flag waving through the night, everything around us suddenly echoing everything else, all of this while north of here hyenas were swarming with flags made of nightmares, swastikas instead of snowflakes, torches lit with hate, on this darkest night of the soul.

Hurricane

Through waves of rain a single window light somewhere across the marsh whispers an intermittent yes and no. Or a far off lighthouse beacon sends a feeble warning. The clanging buoy refuses to reveal its distance. It wants to lean with the tide that is about to change direction. The stained air reveals smudged bruises of light and shadow. It must be the driftwood from the boat that is clambering to climb the rocks. In a while the calm will come and go like a sudden realization rising inside you. Do you think this scene has nothing to do with the refugees who drowned? The eye of the storm always closes before we know what we see.

THE PERSEIDS

A few fireflies seem fooled by the meteors that
slash through the dark like unfinished ideas.
A few lights spark on the corrugated surface
of the water like silver fingerlings. This is the
way mirrors, too, empty themselves of their
secrets. We say the trees point to where the
wind is going as if they chose to do so. This
constellation was originally a Babylonian old
man who lost his way. Now and then the lights
from a plane carry off their own dreams. The
latest theory is that the empty spot in space is
the doorway to another galaxy. So it is we are
carried off by one idea or another as if they were
places to visit.

Desoto State Park, AL

THE GHOSTS AT DAWT MILL

I don't know when the river finally decided to break through the old dam. I don't know when the wind decided to tease the leaves to break from their branches. I don't know why anyone convinced their cells to break away from their necessary duties. I don't know why the stories they wished never happened. We want the river to rush in the opposite direction. We want its ripples to remind us of a lover's caress. We want the light that plays on the surface to tell us whose touch it reveals, something out of a world that could replace this one, a world we could learn to love despite the losses it brings, a world where you look back not in fear or despair, but as if to imagine what the river means by breaking through to a life beyond this one, a life that tells us we are not alone, we are never alone, that every current brings its own beginnings that teach us to love what we cannot see.

Tecumseh, MO

FROM SLOVENIJA

Peace Talks

Their original sentences led nowhere they
meant them to, the wind blowing each word
out of place, the shadows of Napoleons Obelisk
falling as an open wound across the square, and
everywhere the sky emptying itself of itself
while the trajectories of their words, like those
of errant missiles, collide.

Frančiška Trg

Nationalism

A door opens to another mistake, no one
there, only the rain being nothing but rain,
but beyond that everything else is also wrong,
a few metaphors are taken literally, the idea of
the bomb becomes the bomb, but back there,
someone closes the curtain, someone else shuts
the door.

Čopova Ulica

Cafe

There's a note on the table no one has read, and next to it a small espresso cup, empty, sitting in its saucer, the sugar cube never used, the newspaper opened to today's, a world abandoned there by everyone walking by, everyone guilty, everyone refusing to read, to care.

Mestni Trg

Shadows

To step out of your shadow is to step into another time. Lift up the shadow of darkness to see your own darkness. There is always room in your shadow for other shadows. Anyone can draw their own shadow, but only your shadow can draw the dream you shouldn't tell.

Franciscan Church

History

It takes just a few minutes to descend many centuries. Each hunter's spear point holds countless deaths it honors too much to tell. Each artist's shard holds another lost vision. Our words have forgotten their own histories. Our souls are made of clocks. Every artist is a hunter, Tomaž said.

City Museum

Revision

With each night the orb weaver imprisons the same message. With each death the threads of our meanings are cut. Revisions open like black umbrellas deflecting the rain. I watch, instead, while it glistens your urn as Leonard Cohen's recording of IF IT BE YOUR WILL plays against it all.

Metka Krašovec's Funeral

Kosovel

Every poem constructs its own end. An impertinent fog rolls in over the hills. You can hear Kosovel's voice stumbling down the alleyways. Time passes. Or it doesn't. Nothing appears on the painter's canvas, or nothing we can see. Nothing appears on the page except several unreadable symbols and letters.

Kosovel Room, Sežana

Three Letters

1. Note left for Iztok Osojnik from Škocjan, Slovenia

Something steals the sound of the river filling the caverns beneath the town. A few voices guard the cliffs. We want to give these sounds a meaning they don't have. Even the words here seem made of stone. And the stones are dreaming of wings. There's a fault line running through the church like a memory of the prehistoric town. The huge gouges in the earth here were once caves. Someone is still smoking behind a wall where the village women tend their gardens in the sinkholes they call *dolina* that were once ancient burial sites. It was here the partisans hid from the Germans. There are depths here you can only measure by time. The light stammers. In a while I'll be able to smell the stars. A wisp of smoke rises like a question. Then suddenly a voice calls as if from the past. An unwanted memory dives with the falcons out of sight.

2. Note Left for Josh Mensch from Lisbon Portugal

If we trace everything back to the Big Bang then we return to the emptiness we'll become. In Siberia they have uncovered the bones of the Denisovans who no one can explain but who were related to humans. In the end we have to believe in ourselves. The clouds roll up like ancient scrolls. Too often the ruins we leave behind are not enough. Not even this church. Even the sky becomes a dungeon. In the meantime, the sluice gates of horror keep opening like the daily paper, —as with the story of the tortured Bosnian girl, how they placed a live rat in her vagina, and there is none—no response—that makes any sense now, though I want to think our words must be empty in order to be filled, I want to stop these shadows from shivering behind me, I want to forget the news that's flooding the airways with an image of our days,—the child born without a brain, his head a collapsed balloon, his stars long ago become dust, his sky tortured, my own words echoing in the ruins of this church Pessoa must have passed, his own voice trying desperately to fill his lungs.

3. Letter to Ata from the Sedlec Ossuary Church, Kutná Hora, Czech Republic

In the end it doesn't matter whose bones are crossed with yours. What comes after bones is the dream of bones. There's a skull of a small lizard just behind one of the monks. What is missing, you said, is blood. There are 400 miles of blood vessels in the brain, 100 billion neurons. Lin Zhao in prison for 20 years wrote everything in his own blood. All those sense impressions, all those feelings, where do they go when we go? Wycliff's bones were exhumed after twenty years and burned at the stake for heresy not far from here. Paleolithic peoples emptied the brains from skulls then buried the skulls in the center of stone circles to receive the tribe's new dreams. Each of these selves dreamt of being other selves but left no words to tell us who. What do the words in our poems dream when we look away? Only in dreaming a thing does it become real, Ezekial said. Only in silence do we hear what we need to hear.

Six Days: An Italian Journal

Two Galaxies

The woman watches the fire juggler in the piazza below spin twin galaxies from her outstretched arms. The tourists in the piazza don't know she is there. She's not sure herself, living in the distant memory of a memory. Every time she wakes and comes to the window something has disappeared into the broken wormholes of her mind. She half shutters the window. Every word is an invention she's not sure will work. The galaxies merge then split apart. She remembers in that flash the secret word she protected with the other girls, like an ember still trying to glow. The lighted mosaics of the Chiesa Santa Maria hover over everything as if they were beyond this tiny universe. She no longer is sure what it means, but what it means is all the world she has.

—*Piazza Santa Maria, Travestere*

EMERGENCE

The news we are picking up from the star static of the universe is a few billion years old. It seems nothing has changed and we are all heading to an end no one can imagine. I was thinking of this watching the homeless man wrap up his sleeping bag and emerge from behind one of the fragments of wall near the Baths of Caracalla. His shoulder is hunched as if he could feel the sky investigating him. I don't think he knew what to do next. For a moment he turned to walk towards the traffic on Piazzale Numa Pompilio. Even the birdsong sounded like an interrogation. He was too far away to approach. Do you think you know what happened next? You would have to, like him, get on your knees with a rosary and thank the invisible stars for their endless story.

—Baths of Caracalla

ROLES

In the Theater of Marcellus down at the
other end of the street, the executioner's face
was always masked. These ruins tease us with
lessons that have yet to play out. A few gnarled
clouds stalk the sunlight overhead. Chimney
birds rise from their fears. The cats still play on
broken pillars and arches, as they did during
the roundup of October, 1943, and as if there
was nothing special to perform. We too have
been acting in *La Taverna del Ghetto* as if the
Pasta Tartufo was the history we needed. How
easy to keep the plaques and dates on the wall.
The wind recruits a few voices out of sight. We
try to repair with words what words cannot say

—*Rione Sant'Angelo, Rome, Italy*

A MOVABLE WORLD

The early doves have already started to harvest the light. Without permits, the Sudanese men fold their cardboard tables up like wings as the Carbinieri approach from the shadows. Their rings and scarfs are anchored to the surface as they will never be. A language of gestures and signs from the other end of the street has warned them. Jeans, imitation leather jacket, Converse shoes, their names too are fluid to their handlers. But there is one who pauses to glance back, older, whose gaze doesn't leave when he does. After a while, it chips away at the air, chips away at the heart's flint. The light, now, has stopped looking for a prey.

—*Florence*

TRAIN

When you ride backwards on a train memories rise like that flock of quail at the hunter's approach. Centuries ago the painters here put their own friends and landscapes in historical pictures as a way to defeat time. The distance to termini is just a few half read newspapers. Farms and towns shrink into their names. There is a belief that this is when you realize your life, too, shrinks into its name. Outside the window a few fanatics think they are making history. But there is no history, only this future we back into not quite as blindly as we want.

—*Between Florence and Rome*

Belief

From here the world still looks upside down. The news records the blossoming silence after the bomb goes off. Words vaporize. There's a new honor killing someone tries to sell as love or religion. Below here, even the cemeteries try to shrug off despair. Maybe time is the lizard emerging from the cracks in the stone wall. If I didn't know better I'd say it was emerging from a dream that died here long ago. The courtyard pigeons grumble at anyone who doesn't believe. And anxious wind tugs at the Peter's sign. I think the old man against the wall must be him, must know what is coming as he tries to brush away the first stars with a wave of his wand.

—*San Pietro in Montoio, Travestere, Rome*

LJUBLJANA DIARY

Afterward as Prelude

Whenever we return it is a different place. The hills, the streets, no longer recognize us. The geese, the constellations arrive as expected. Our own memories are refugees from a world that no longer exists. The future sits at her window watching Wolfova Street below. A cat is stalking a better life at a drainpipe. Every gust of wind has a story it won't tell. We have to invent the town in order to see it. We have to invent the soul in order to speak of it.

20 November

BRIDGES

The cloud shadows seems to flap in the light breeze as if to signal some mythic meaning. The tiny bird at my table twists its neck like a curious child waiting for the future to explain what she is seeing. I think these birds bring news from beyond whatever horizon we could imagine. Something like the dragon statues on the bridge who seem to appear through the thin skin of the past. Or the padlocks on the next bridge left to lock away the rubble of countless dreams. On the triple bridge there is a bench half way on the middle span where the young guitar player is singing a lament for only being able to take one span at a time. Here the past is a myth because it is always rewritten as the present, and for this the shadows keep drawing our latest lives.

8 November

BORDERS

The hawk that circles above the castle must be hunting for a lost past. There are Roman dreams here still waiting to be realized. The late light razors across the tops of buildings. East of here the refugees believe a future made of geography, but there are borders no map dare show. The world they came from is made of sawdust. Every speck of dust hides its own vision, Tomaž would say. All it needs is a little window made of light. Every word is an escape rope thrown out of one of those windows The road to the castle is not the one that spirals around the hill. The words of the heart are not the ones we meant to build. This has nothing or everything to do with the homeless man sleeping in the castle hill bushes whose dream is the cry of a single, wingless bird.

9 November

Construction Project

It's true there is another city behind this one. They are connected by an intricate thread of mistranslated events. There, our other lives manage what we could not do here. There is no way in but only a way out across a bridge we are never allowed to build. It is marked by the dog-eared corner of our dreams. There are signs of course—the old woman under the three rivers column talking to the ground fog, the way the child on the tricycle weaves in and out of what we thought were empty spaces on the river walk, the way another child chases pigeons from Trubar Street into a world only he sees, even the way we ourselves feel it necessary to walk among the empty stalls of the marketplace at 2 AM. Could this be it? Could it finally happen? Or will we never escape the burden of knowing we live in the shadows of a constantly constructed truth?

10 November

The New Calculus

Light rustles against the curb. You have to watch your step. You don't want to trip over the rope of shadows the dog trails behind him. Who knows what that would lead to? We die too many times each day to compute the answer. The question is, where do we go during those times? The meaning of the sky's tattoos is unclear. Above Prešeren Square they are hanging Christmas stars and also meteorites just to make the universe seem complete. When we saw the comet years ago it hardly seemed to move. In Giotto's fresco of the stigmata the blood lines create a geometry that links heaven and earth. It took us a long time to solve the equation. Then we ate falafel at the late night stand on Copova Street.

11 November

Autumn Fog

A few birds guard the chimney tops waiting for clarity. Another has slapped the window amazed to have met himself that way. Everything is in disguise. North of here a few peaks breach the surface. Some types of birds will fly in ever narrowing circles to approach their invisible roosts. The backup warning of the delivery truck seems to sound from everywhere. It is as if we were waiting for the world to surface, waiting for the net to bring up its bounty. Or we are all spiraling down towards something we can't see. We have just a few words for a compass. It seems the roads here lead to the end of time. East of here a group of refugees pray for the fog to hold them safe for the night.

12 November

THE BELLS

The mountain pastures drape down around the church. Here the Kamnick Alps have already relaxed their hold on summer. Pockets of light were already emptying themselves of loose fog. The distant rock faces say how difficult it is to reach the sky. Even the church is locked. At least all this will survive us, someone says. From the village far below a church bell seems to climb towards us. It is a long way, through the smells of manure and pine, but we are patient for we had already determined it was not the clanging in our own hearts.

13 November

WAKING TO NEWS FROM PARIS

What dispatches the river brings make no
sense. As when you try to understand the words
by the shape of breath on the cold air. As when
a dream casts is mangled shadow onto the light.
The air is suddenly empty, the dawn reluctant
to be dawn. Suddenly the lingering stars no
longer seem eternal. The light on Novi Square
defies the ground fog. Above it, the crescent
moon wants to change its shape. In the space
of a few sentences countless words have died.
The real terror is getting used to pain the way
the rocks accept the slow erosion of the river.

14 November

POSTSCRIPT

This morning's sky is more fragile than ever. Jupiter and Mars keep stalking Venus. A spider web nods as if it understood what the whispering wind was trying to tell it. There's a hovering fly that doesn't know it's out of season. Lights squint from the far hills pretending to be lost stars. So too the barbs in the border fences. There is so much we can't connect. Isn't it amazing how easily we create little boxes to live inside? It seems as if even the city doves on the windowsills expect an answer.

19 November

THE SCALE OF THINGS:
HAIBUN SEQUENCE

Montgomery Elegy

When another truck drives into a crowd or
another village suffocates with gas, time slips
its hood over what happens and we trudge on
into a future that is perhaps given in the figure
of the laughing girl, skinny jeans, embroidered
t-shirt taking a selfie with her friends in front of
the King Church which is itself as out of focus
as our histories, and when she bends over to
retrieve her lip gloss I see, for a moment, an old
woman's bent spine years from now, trying to
remember where that photo was taken, though,
watching her, who am I, each self refusing to
speak to
      the other, living
      as I am in a crowd of
      broken compasses.

Syrian Elegy

A first light shoots through the holes in the
wall. To simply name what's left of the family
that the light tracks towards is to cheapen their
memory. Their own names hover above them in
the smoke. The shadows darting in and out of
the buildings below have no idea. Someone fires
over a broken wall without looking. Another
has sat down, shaking, for he has lost control.
He is not even embarrassed. It is a knowledge
like the sound of the missile that appears later
than the impact. He is focused on a deflated
soccer ball he mistook for crushed squash. The
dust keeps kicking up as if it wanted to escape
as a cloud. No one pays attention to the slogans
that blow by like dried leaves.

> The words of distant
> negotiators hover
> as high as their drones.

THE SCALE OF THINGS

Even the wind spits its protests between the words of this poem. The bats clinging to their branches must be afraid to return to their caves. Even in darkness the shadow of the great horned owl knifing towards the vole seems visible. I remember the boy asking why the deer would be riddled with so many holes. But that is nothing compared to what happens to a body. And that is nothing compared to the shadow of a missile where in Ghouta Syria, the mother who had been baking scraps of cornmeal and barley bread, prays for

>the shadow that is
>the soul of her son: *at least*
>*there's food in heaven.*

Near Tucson

The heavy light holds everything in place,
trees, clouds, words, the distant highway hum.
Even our dreams seem locked safely away. For
a moment it seems like we could lose nothing.
The old stories seem painted on the air. The
ancient wall paintings have refused centuries
of weather. There are scuffed tracks here whose
age we cannot know. *Pollos*, is what they call
them, the name they give to those who walked
from far south of here to nowhere they could
walk.

> Coyotes begin
> to rub now against the wall
> of the coming dusk.

Two Worlds

Tonight the wolf moon seems bright enough
to show us how we have been hunted by time,
how often our own dreams are devoured by
their own shadows, how often our lives are
emptied of other lives, lost lives inside of other
lost lives. Even the insects seem to have lost
their breath. The lamp light wavers between
yes and no. Tomaž stood once in the dim light
of the main chamber in Postojna Caves, arms
outstretched, spinning like a weather vane,
and dipping now and then like the branches
of a tree in the wind, and singing how we are
already pointing towards imagined worlds
beyond the walls. We are, he said, like the blind
human fish that live there and see more than we
ever will. In truth, he was already buried, as we
all were, in an earth that gladly welcomes us
back. Tonight, packs of shadows seem to stalk
us under the swaying trees. The light signals a
warning to the moon while the moon seems to
whisper another in return, something about the
eternity the he came to face exactly as it came
to face him, revealed tonight when

> tassels of pampas
> grass sway against the lamplight—
> his returning breath.

The End of the Story

*More than the midpoint between homegrown and
anglo their tongue is a nebulous territory between
what is dying out and what is not yet born...a
shrewd metamorphosis, a self-defensive shift. It's not
another way of saying things: these are new things.
The world happening anew...promising other things,
signifying other things....*

> —Yuri Herrera, *Signs Preceding the End of
> the World*

Or why he came to sit in that hypothetical
landscape only the next few words would tell.
If only he could find the right tense, for around
him Time seemed always to be updating itself.
And yet the more he wrote the more Time itself
became meaningless. The moment's borders
between past and future appeared like a mirage
on the desert floor, if indeed that's where he
was. He wrote the word cactus simply to assure
himself. He wrote a word for where he wanted
to be though it was always changing,

> but he could hear trees
> flex a few millimeters
> up towards the word *sky*

see the stars detach,
silently drifting, fading
from his dream of sky

the way the children, detached from their
parents despite what he wanted to write,
despite the way the past seemed to persist in his
marginal notes, but what could he write that
was true and not a mirage of the border, not
simply the delirium of the wind against his face,
not simply an archaic meaning he never knew,
not certainly a word that was itself thinking *do
not stop thinking of me before I deport you into a
language you cannot read.*

Unsaying:
Meditations from
Slovenia

NEVER THERE

Soča Valley, Izonzo Front in 1917

They are hesitant, the buds, barely visible on the lime trees. They seem to know what emptiness they will replace. They seem to know history is a faded watermark. The road collects its own past with each hesitating hairpin turn. We are here as part of an ongoing litany but can't confirm that now. The hawk that watches me suspiciously from a branch above the soldiers' graveyard waits for a mouse to emerge from under the ground cover to reveal itself. Each soldier here knew a moment that stretched one life into another. It always seems to come after the fact. There is no truth, even in that moment. By now the evening that seemed to take forever to begin fills with clouds that tell the first stars to wait, be cautious for what comes next. It is a moment when everything remembers what was never there as something that will always be there.

MIXED METAPHORS FOR WHO KNOWS WHAT

Raku Škocjan

The river here grinds down the sandstone into a past we have forgotten and tells a future we'll never know. The natural stone bridges are doorways filled with doorways. These are stories that never resolve themselves on their own. There are no antecedents for the pronouns though we get some picture of where they are headed. Beyond, an unseen town hovers over the ridge where the evergreens stand stark black against a red sky. Someone always expects something of us. The wind is trying to tally the results. We try to read the stars but they don't know anymore than we do. The walls of the cliffs assert traces from epoch to epoch. There's something I want to ask but my words outpace their meanings. That's when the fox drifts out of the woods as if he knew what I was thinking.

WORDLESS

Mlino, Lake Bled

It was a night where there were only words that had no meaning. At first they seemed to float like pollen through the dream. Then they were stars. Then like the flashlights of searchers lacing through the woods except there were no woods. No stars or pollen either, but like them. How long had I lay there? I could almost hear an owl question the status of certain stars but by then I was waking. Was he in the dream or in the woods? There was a war and then there wasn't. The whole place seemed a façade to hide a broken sky. There are whole lists we are not privy to. The reeds coming out of the water, I now see, were only a distraction. Someone else stops on the opposite shore because he hears something. He is made of the same dream of atoms as I am. His words are taking forever to reach me. How long has it been? What were the lights searching for? Then, suddenly, I am older and no longer myself.

Temperature Inversion

Postojna

These tress tell us there is no place we are
safe. Wind, then ice, have whittled away the
tops or decapitated them, cracked them like
arthritic bones. But why these metaphors that
steal what they try to name and understand?
There is a whole realm of being that is beyond
them for *whittle, decapitated* and *bones* make
them human and hide the loss of light that
shaded and formed each leaf or needle, how
those drew water to make sap, and how a
whole world of nests, worms, insects, bacteria,
entangled systems disappeared. We ourselves
are metaphors for what we can't do. Trees and
ideals collapse. We want a world that is easier
to understand. But now these new leaves have
not known another life and, regardless of the
future, pay no attention to mine or anyone's
words for them.

THE HIDDEN

Cernoko, the Disappearing Lake

It is all limestone here, porous, where the lake
disappears into another world beneath this
one like a nest in the hollow of a tree. It is
here even when it isn't. It's a question of belief.
Of faith. One time, as a boy, I tried to hold
a shaft of sunlight like a spear that had come
through my bedroom window. What we see
is already something else. After the Big Bang,
the universe went dark not even believing in
itself, just bubbles of ionized gas, until the first
stars emerged. That is always the way. Night
gathers in pools by the roadside. They hold
within them galaxies of other times and places.
It was Jason and the Argonauts who must have
figured the world was shrinking back into one
atom when they visited here. After it didn't,
they invented another theory. This is the case
with every belief, disappearing into itself, into
whatever it is we believe we saw.

MISSING

Ljubljana

It is as if you could see the buried city beneath
this one the way we used to look at our bones
by holding a light behind our hands, or the way
those old x-ray machines for measuring shoe
size revealed a body we didn't know. Beneath
me stirs the Roman town of Emona where I
imagine a blacksmith trying to imagine what
dreams we forge. They don't get any better. An
express train drags the past through the station.
The news today is all abduction, shifting
borders and pillage. What we don't know
is fast approaching. What we thought were
harmless ideas turned out to be accomplices.
The streetlights are never bright enough. At
such times we are all missing. Sometimes the
truth is the nature we hide from ourselves. It is
buried beneath the silt of our words. It is is not
a question of archeology as we had imagined.

HISTORY

Ptuj

The body doesn't know what to do with its
discarded feelings. They stand like broken
columns the Romans left just breaking into
consciousness above the grass line. In the
distance, the moon burrows into a mountain,
the sky turns into earth. In a little while we'll be
living in the marrow of darkness. They used to
think lighthouses were the answer until pirates
lit false fires on the rocks. The heart, someone
said, is a grifter. We are all dark matter. No
one knows where our stories came from. In
the center of town Orpheus' monument is
powerless to resurrect anything. All there is
now is his voiceless light. The ancient trade
routes have changed direction. There are too
many erasures here to count. The body knows
what beats in the heart is not the heart but
hearts.

Praprotnikova 5

It is being,...quickened to the point of receiving...
or hearkening...within itself, in the intelligible and
super-intelligible integrity of the tone particular to
it.

    —Jacques Maritain, *Existence and the Existent*

Halos of mist wrap around the streetlights.
Every sound is pocketed. Birds who think they
are angels wonder why there are no answers for
what they sing. Dusk begins to sift through the
mist. The woman with the shopping cart who
passed by a moment ago calls out from the
next street and someone answers, but not to
her. There are no angels here. The halos quiver.
A single bird drinks from a street puddle. The
sky leans down onto the shoulders of buildings.
She calls out again. This is the source of her
perfect love. It may or may not be a question
of theology.

Vipava Valley

The historian looks backwards, and finally he believes backwards.

—Nietzsche

Legions of rain troop through the valley. Near here in 394 the Romans fought to divide their empire, and did. Cobwebs begin to glisten under the eaves. A few townsfolk open their umbrellas as if to create their own horizons. The thunder advances into its own echo. The calendar we have been checking curls up from the damp. Nothing wants to stay as it is. Whatever words we had for this have always already spilled down the gutters, searching. The Battlefield was never found. I'm not sure if the roads are safe. Tomorrow retreats into the cliffs to escape our plans.

About the Author

Richard Jackson is the author of 19 books of poetry including *Where The Wind Comes From*, *Broken Horizons* and *The Heart as Framed: New & Select Poems*, and 12 books of essays, interviews, translations and anthologies. He was awarded the Order of Freedom Medal for literary and humanitarian work during the Balkan wars by the President of Slovenia during his work with the Slovene-based Peace and Sarajevo Committees of PEN International. He has received Guggenheim, Fulbright, NEA, NEH, and two Witter-Bynner fellowships, a *Prairie Schooner* Reader's Choice Award, and the Crazyhorse prize, and he is the winner of five Pushcart Prizes and has appeared in *Best American Poems* as well as many other anthologies.

ALSO BY RICHARD JACKSON

Poems

Where The Wind Comes From

Broken Horizons (Silver Conch Selection)

Take Five (with 4 other poets)

Resonancia (Barcelona)

Out of Place (Franklin Award)

Traversings (with Robert Vivian)

Retrievals (Maxine Kumin Award)

Resonance (Eric Hofer Award)

Half Lives: Petrarchan Poems

Unauthorized Autobiography

Alive All Day (Cleveland State Award)

Falling Stars (Limited Edition)

Svetovi Narazen (Slovenia)

Heart's Bridge (Limited Edition)

Heartwall (Juniper Prize)

Worlds Apart (Univ. Alabama Press Selection)

Part of the Story

The Heart as Framed: New & Select Poems
(Press 53)

Translations

Last Poems: Selected Poems of Giovanni Pascoli
(Italian, with Susan Thomas, Deborah Brown)

Potovanje Sonca (Journey of the Sun) *by*
Alexsander Peršola (Slovene)

Chapbooks

Strays

Fifties

Cesare Pavese: The Woman in the Land
(translation)

Greatest Hits 1980-2004

Critical Books and Editions

*Dismantling Time in Contemporary American
Poetry*

Acts of Mind: Interviews with American Poets

The Fire Under the Moon

The Heart's Many Doors

Double Vision: Slovene Poetry

Iztok Osojnik: Selected Poems